Contents

D1471112

All the words that appear in
bold are explained in
the glossary on page 30.

Plastics are everywhere

Look around the room now. How many things can you see that are made from plastics? Many of these objects would be difficult to make using other materials like wood, metal or clay.

Plastics are useful because they are tough, waterproof, light, easily cleaned, hard-wearing and cheap to produce. They do not rust or rot, they **insulate** well and they can be made into any shape. For these reasons plastics are used to make many of the everyday objects we use at home such as baths, toys, light switches, lunch boxes and garden chairs.

You may find that many of your toys and games are made from plastics.

4

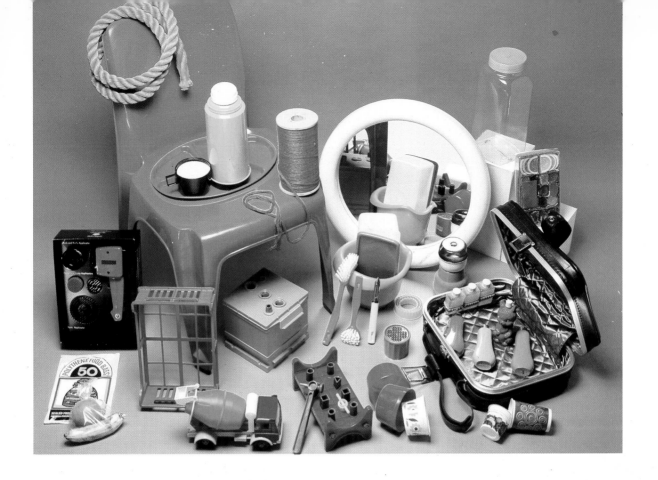

Plastics also have important uses in medicine. Plastic parts are used in many operations like hip replacements and for making tiny heart **pacemakers** which help to keep people's hearts beating. They can even be used to make false teeth!

Many people once thought of plastics as cheap and not very good quality. Today we can produce high quality plastics which look good as well as being useful.

Some of the everyday objects found in the home that are made of plastics.

5

The first plastics

Wood, metal, silk and clay have been used to make things for thousands of years. The first plastics were made only about 130 years ago so plastics are a very recent invention.

One of the early types of plastic was invented in Britain. It was called celluloid and was used instead of ivory to make billiard balls. Soon toys were made of celluloid too. Perhaps the most important use of celluloid was to make film for cinema cameras. But today it is used mostly to make ping-pong balls.

Today celluloid is used to make ping-pong balls.

The use of electricity in our homes also relies on plastics. Wires and light switches need to be insulated so that people do not get electric shocks. Another early plastic, invented by Dr Baekland, was called Bakelite. It was often used to insulate electrical equipment.

Bakelite plastic was used to make early radios, cameras and boxes.

So, we can see that in a short time plastics have become a very important part of our lives. Without them, many everyday inventions might not have been discovered.

The origins of plastics

To begin with, plastics were only made from things found in nature in their raw form. Would you have thought that plastic could be made from cow's milk? Scientists took out a special substance from the milk. This substance was washed, dried, ground up, coloured, shaped and hardened into plastic. This plastic was then used to make buttons, jewellery and suitcases.

A popular use for early plastics was to make colourful buttons in many shapes.

Plastics were also made from coal, cotton, wood, animal horn and rubber. Today the most important raw materials for making plastics are oil and natural gas. There are large stores of these resources buried deep underground all over the world. Not so long ago it would have been very difficult to dig them out. Now we use huge drills which can reach supplies of oil and gas quite easily.

Scientists have invented many new types of plastic using oil and gas. These have much wider uses than the early plastics.

Above *The first plastics were made from milk, coal, cotton and wood.*

Below *Oil is now the most important raw material for producing plastics.*

Turning oil into plastics

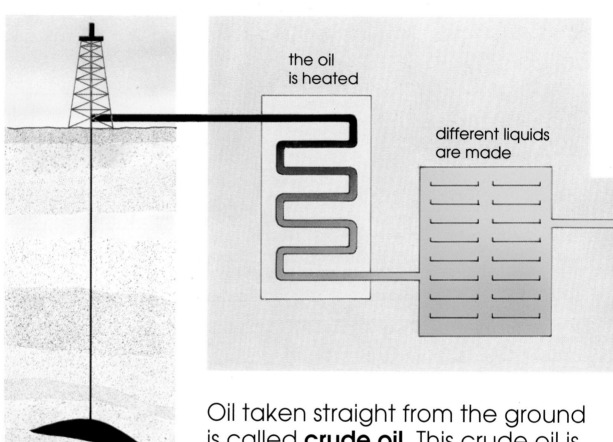

the oil
is heated

different liquids
are made

the oil is drilled

This diagram shows how crude oil is turned into plastic chips.

Oil taken straight from the ground is called **crude oil**. This crude oil is sent to an oil refinery, which is like a giant factory. Here, the oil is heated up in a big tower called a **fractionating tower.** The heat turns it into several different types of liquid. These are used to make petrol for cars, diesel oil for lorries and paraffin for lamps. The liquid needed for plastics, called **naphtha**, is also produced. This is piped away separately.

Chemists then heat the liquid naphtha again to make a substance called ethylene. From this, thousands of tiny pieces of plastic are produced. They are called **polyethylene chips** and look a bit like white gravel. The diagram shows how the whole process happens.

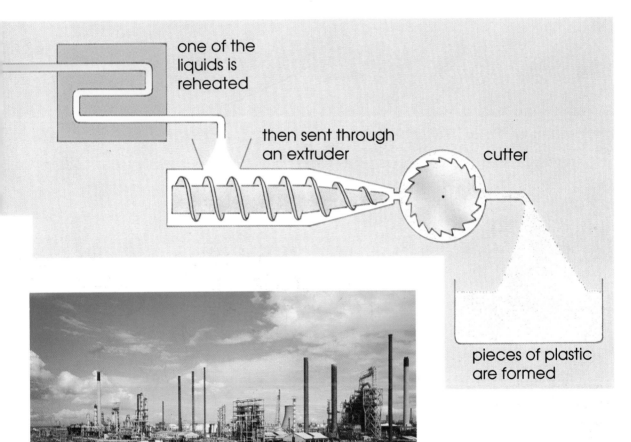

one of the liquids is reheated

then sent through an extruder

cutter

pieces of plastic are formed

Left A modern oil refinery can be the size of a small town!

11

Making plastic shapes

Plastics can be moulded into any shape to make toys like these.

Once the plastic chips have been produced they are ready to be shaped into plastic objects. There are several ways this can be done.

One method is called **extrusion**. The plastic chips are melted and the hot plastic is squeezed through a specially-shaped hole by an extruder. This is like a giant mincer. When the plastic cools and hardens it makes long, hollow tubes. These can be used for making such things as water pipes or guttering.

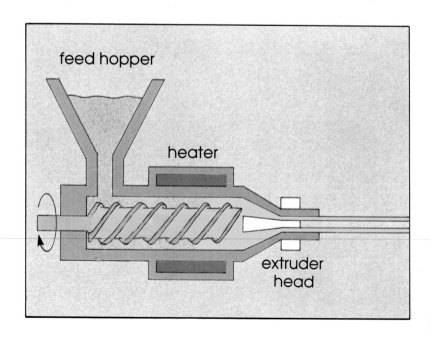

feed hopper

heater

extruder head

Plastic chips are fed through an extruder to make long, hollow tubes of plastic.

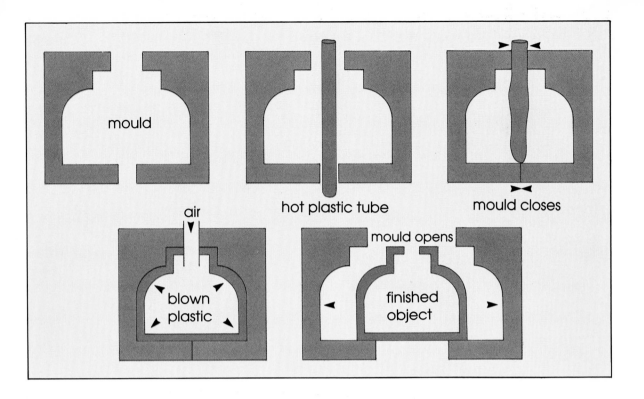

mould

hot plastic tube

mould closes

air

blown plastic

mould opens

finished object

Another way of shaping plastics is called **moulding**. Again the plastic chips are melted and then forced into a specially-shaped mould. Air is blown into the mould rather like blowing up a balloon. This presses the hot plastic against the sides of the mould.

When the plastic has cooled and hardened, the mould is split open. The finished object has now taken up the same shape as the mould and is hollow inside. Plastic bottles, toys and footballs can all be made by this method.

This diagram shows how melted plastics are moulded into shapes by blowing air through them.

Making plastic sheets

A greenhouse made from perspex sheets.

Sheets of thick, hard plastic are also made by extrusion or moulding. **Perspex** is a thick plastic and is very useful because it is see-through and does not break as easily as glass. It can be used for the canopies of aircraft or as the windowpanes of greenhouses.

Thin sheets, or films of plastic are made in a different way. This process is called **calendering**.

Moulded perspex is very strong and ideal for aircraft canopies.

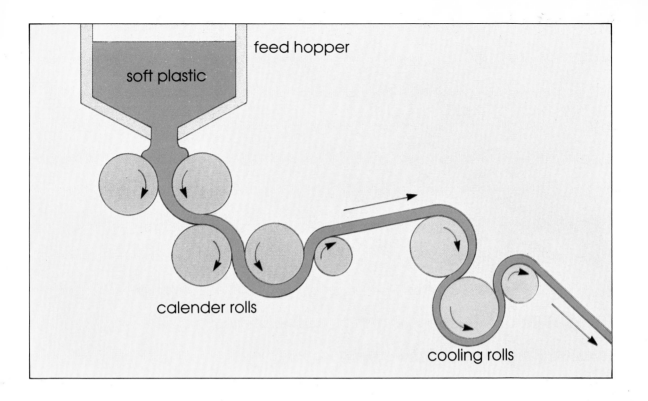

feed hopper

soft plastic

calender rolls

cooling rolls

Plastic chips are melted and allowed to cool slightly. While the plastic is still soft and bendy it is fed through a line of rollers which looks rather like an old-fashioned clothes mangle. These press the plastic into long, flat sheets which are hardened again by cold air.

Thin sheets of plastic are made by squeezing soft plastic between giant rollers.

Plastic sheets have many uses. They can be cut up to make shopping bags or used to keep out the damp underneath new houses. Very thin films of plastic are used to wrap food and keep it fresh.

Making plastic foam

Plastic can also be produced as a foam. Foam is made by blowing gas into melted plastic. The bubbles of gas make the plastic get bigger. Very hard slabs of plastic can be made in this way. These slabs are lightweight but very strong. They can be used to insulate buildings or to make solid parts of furniture.

Soft, bendy plastic foam can also be made into soft furniture parts. In the past these could produce very poisonous smoke if they accidentally caught fire. For this reason furniture foam now has to be as fireproof as possible.

Blocks of polystyrene foam are used to insulate buildings.

16

Polystyrene is an example of plastic foam. It is usually white and it is cheap, lightweight and insulates well. It is often used to make cups and dishes for packaging take-away food. It is also good for insulating and soundproofing walls of buildings. Little beads of polystyrene are often used as packing around fragile objects.

The air bubbles in plastic foam make it strong but lightweight. This picture shows what plastic foam looks like under a microscope.

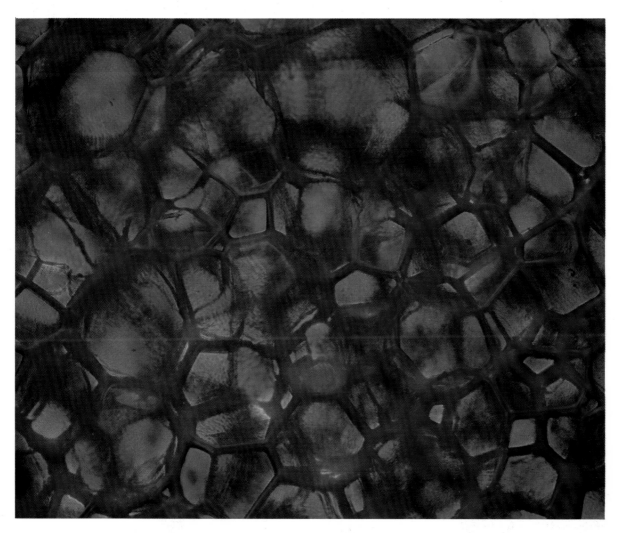

Making plastic clothes

We have seen how sheets of plastic are made. These can be turned into clothes such as plastic raincoats. The plastic sheet is cut into the right shapes by machines and then sewn or **heat-sealed** together. The plastic can be coloured with dyes before it is rolled into sheets which makes it much brighter and more fun to wear.

Above *The seams of plastic clothes are heat-sealed together.*

Right *Plastic raincoats can be made in bright colours that are fun to wear.*

This spinneret machine is producing threads of plastic which will be used to knit or weave clothes.

Another way plastics are used is to make fibres or **yarn** for clothes. These fibres are woven or knitted together. Plastic chips are melted and then forced through hundreds of tiny holes in a **spinneret**. This looks like the funnel on the end of a watering can. Long threads of plastic come out of the other end. They are cooled and hardened, then stretched and wound together to make acrylic, nylon and many other **synthetic** fibres.

Plastic paints and glues

All sorts of modern paints contain plastics, for example **emulsion paint** for walls and **gloss paint** for windows and doors. When the paint dries the plastic gives it a very tough and hard-wearing surface which can easily be wiped clean with a damp cloth.

This decorator is using paint containing plastics which will give it strength and make it last a long time.

20

Plastic acrylic paint is very quick-drying and the brushes can be easily cleaned after use. Today, artists often use acrylic paint instead of oil paint.

Plastics are also used in many modern glues to make them strong and waterproof. Some glues come in two tubes – a resin and a hardener. When the contents of the tubes are mixed, chemicals react which harden the glue and give it the strength to stick things together.

Another kind of glue is often called super-glue. The plastic in this makes it so strong that it can stick a man to the wing of an aeroplane – while it is flying!

Modern glues dry quickly and stick very firmly because of the plastics they contain.

Plastics in the future

Every year new plastics are invented: special plastics for spaceships, plastics which protect fire-fighters from fires and plastics which can even mend themselves if they are split.

As we have seen throughout this book, plastics have thousands of uses. But can you imagine what you would do without them? What would you use to carry your lunch to school if you did not have your plastic lunch box?

New plastics are always being invented. Many of them are used in space rockets.

22

At the moment there is plenty of oil and gas to make into plastics. Some countries, like the USSR, have large stores of these resources but need help from scientists in other countries to make them into plastics.

Racing drivers can now wear special plastic suits that protect them from fire.

The world's reserves of oil and gas cannot last forever. Coal could be used to make plastics but this would be expensive. Scientists may invent ways to make new sorts of plastics without oil. Or, perhaps we might go back to using materials like wood, metal and clay again.

Plastics and pollution

On average, every person produces about 23 kg of plastic waste each year. Many plastic objects, such as plastic bottles and food packaging, are made to be thrown away after use.

Unlike paper or wood, most plastics **decompose** very slowly. This is harmful to our environment because it causes **pollution**. Rivers and sea-shores are often littered with plastic waste.

Food packaging often contains plastics, which are thrown away after use.

One answer may be to make more objects from **biodegradable** plastic. When these are buried, they are broken down by **bacteria** in the soil. Another answer could be **photodegradable** plastic which is broken down by sunlight. However, the best answer to the plastics waste problem is to **recycle** materials.

Throwing away plastic is very wasteful. Many countries in Europe and the USA have built special factories to burn plastic waste and turn it into electricity. To do this the plastic waste must be separated from the other rubbish. This could be more easily done if every household separated their glass, tins, paper and plastic. It would then be easier to recycle.

Plastic waste pollutes much of our environment especially around rivers and sea-shores.

Recycling plastics

There are many ways to recycle plastics. Many countries have started plastic bottle banks where people can dump their plastic containers just like glass bottle banks. They can then be processed into new products. These include plastic fibres for clothes, sleeping-bags and special bricks to burn as fuel.

Some fizzy drinks companies now make plastic bottles which can be returned and re-used.

These bottle banks in the USA are used to collect glass, plastic bottles and aluminium cans for recycling.

Many shops all over the world sell plastic rubbish bags which have been made out of recycled plastic. They also give recycled carrier bags to their customers to carry home their shopping.

Separating plastic waste from other rubbish so that it can be recycled.

However, there is a much simpler way to reuse plastic. We could all try to break the habit of using new plastic bags each time we go shopping. If everyone took old plastic bags with them to the supermarket a lot of waste would be saved.

Projects with plastics

Make a model glider

You will need:

A polystyrene food tray
A craft knife

Plasticine
Pen and paper

1. Design a model glider. Draw the glider to size on a piece of paper. You will need one shape for the body, one for the wings and one for the tail wings as shown below.

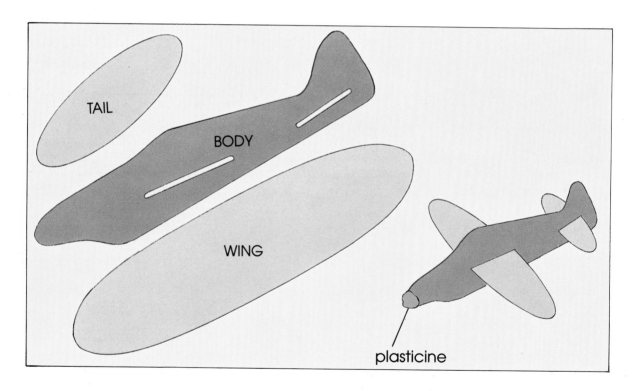

TAIL

BODY

WING

plasticine

2. Cut your shapes out and draw them on to the polystyrene tray. With an adult to help you, cut out the polystyrene using a craft knife. Make a slit for the wings and tail, and push them through.

3. You will need to balance your glider before you fly it. Place the tips of the wings on the backs of two chairs. If the tail drops, add some plasticine to the nose to balance it.

Test the strength of plastics

You will need:

A variety of plastic bags
Sandpaper

Water
Clock or watch

1. Collect together a variety of plastic bags and rub each one gently with sandpaper until it tears.

Make a note of how long it takes for a hole to appear in each of the bags.

2. Or try filling plastic bags full of water until they break. Always hold them over a bath or basin.

Make a note of how much water the bags will hold before they break.

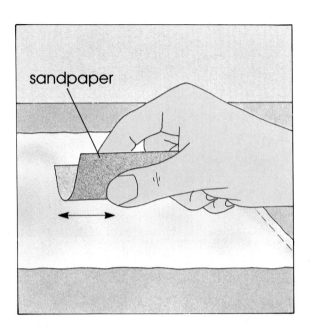

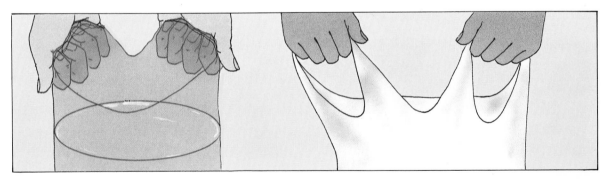

For whichever experiment you decided to do, you could put your results under one of the headings in a table like this:

	Number of seconds to make hole	Number of cups of water to break
BAG 1		
BAG 2		
BAG 3		

Glossary

Bacteria   Tiny living organisms which can break down waste.

Biodegradable   Something that can be broken down by bacteria when it has been buried in the earth.

Calendering   A way of rolling hot plastic to make it into flat sheets.

Crude oil   Oil which is straight from the ground and has not been treated.

Decompose   To be broken down by bacteria.

Emulsion paint   A dull paint used to paint walls.

Extrusion   A way of making very long pieces of plastic like water pipes or guttering.

Fractionating tower   A very tall tower where oil is heated.

Gloss paint   Shiny, hard-wearing paint used to paint woodwork.

Heat-sealed   Plastic that has been stuck together using heat.

Insulate   To keep heat inside or protect from electric shock.

Moulding   A way of making hollow plastic objects. The object takes on the same shape as the mould.

Naphtha   The name given to the liquid from crude oil that is used to make plastics.

Pacemakers   Tiny plastic batteries that help weak hearts to beat strongly.

Perspex   A thick, see-through type of plastic and a trade name for acrylic sheets.

Photodegradable   Something that can be broken down by sunlight.

Pollution   Damage caused to the environment by waste products.

Polyethylene chips   Tiny pieces of plastic that look like white gravel.

Polystyrene   A lightweight plastic used for packaging and to make cups to be thrown away.

Recycle   To use something again or to change it into something new.

Spinneret   A machine that has lots of small holes, like the head of a shower. Hot plastic is forced through the small holes to make thin threads.

Synthetic   Something that humans have made and that is not found in nature.

Yarn   Fibres of wool, cotton or plastic made into thread.

Books to read

Cash, T. **Plastics** (A & C Black, 1989)
Graham, A. **Let's go to an Oil Rig** (Young Library, 1986)
Harness, A. **The Story of Plastics** (Ladybird Books, 1972)
Horne, M. **Children and Plastics** (Macdonald Educational, 1978)
Jackman, W. **Plastic Raincoat** (Wayland, 1990)
Lambert, M. **Focus on Plastics** (Wayland, 1987)
Whyman, K. **Plastics** (Franklin Watts, 1987)

Useful addresses

Australia
Australian Association for
   Environmental Education
GPO Box 112
Canberra, ACT 2601

Canada
Canadian Plastics Institute
1262 Don Mills Road
Toronto, Ontario
M3B 2W7

Friends of the Earth (Canada)
Suite 53
54 Queen Street
Ottawa, KP5CS

UK
BP Plastics Education Service
c/o Blackburn Compact Business
   Centre
Faynom Wharfe
Blackburn BB1 5BN

The British Plastics Federation
5 Belgrave Square
London SW1X 8PD

Wellman International Ltd
(PET Bottle Recycling)
Mullagh, Kells
Co Meath
Republic of Ireland

Index

Picture acknowledgements

The publishers would like to thank the following for allowing their photographs to be reproduced in this book: Paul Brierley *cover* (top), 17; Bruce Coleman Ltd (Michael Freeman) 14 (bottom); (R. Carr) 16; E. T. Archive 7; Eye Ubiquitous (Paul Seheult) 8 and 21, 24 (J. Winkley) 26; Robert Harding *cover* (bottom), *title page*; Hutchison 27; Topham 23; Wayland Picture Library (Zul Mukhida) 4; (Shell) 5 (top), (Tim Woodcock) 6, (Chris Fairclough) 9 (top), (Shell) 9 (bottom), 11 and 19, (Paul Seheult) 12, (Chris Fairclough) 18 (both), (Shell) 19; (Angus Blackburn) 25; Zefa Picture Library (G. Mabbs) 14 (top), 20, 22. All illustrations by Jenny Hughes.